Williamsburg

Williamsburg
A Seasonal Sampler

Photography by David M. Doody

Text by Thad W. Tate

Colonial Williamsburg
The Colonial Williamsburg Foundation
Williamsburg, Virginia

16 15 14 13 12 11 10 09   6 7 8 9 10

Library of Congress
Cataloging-in-Publication Data

Doody, David M.
    Williamsburg : a seasonal sampler / photography
by David M. Doody ; text by Thad W. Tate.
        p.   cm.
    ISBN 0-87935-168-3
    1. Williamsburg (Va.)—Pictorial works. I. Tate,
Thad W.
II. Colonial Williamsburg Foundation. III. Title
F234.W7D66   1996
975.5'4252—dc20   96-32103
                                    CIP

ISBN-13: 978-0-87935-168-7

This book was designed by Helen M. Olds

Printed in China

The Colonial Williamsburg Foundation
PO Box 1776
Williamsburg, VA 23187-1776
www.colonialwilliamsburg.org

Seasons of Light

Of all the tools of the trade at the command of a Colonial Williamsburg photographer—the selection of lenses, the electronic cameras, the digital darkrooms—it may be that none is more useful than the ordinary paradox.

A paradox, of course, is a sort of play on words, a seemingly contradictory statement that nonetheless is true and often very serviceable. Here's one I carry, like my camera bag, to every assignment: My job is to see this old and immutable city in a new and ever-changing light.

Light is the pivot on which the paradox turns. Photography is mainly about light, about using it to shape, to color, and to define the scenes and subjects in the lens.

Light changes minute by minute, day to day, season after season. Its quality differs with the sun's height and angle, with the hours, and with the solstices and equinoxes that shepherd in spring and fall, summer and winter. It is constant only in its inconstancy; at one extreme as diffuse as a sunset filtered through the haze of a Tidewater day in August; at the other as crystalline as a crisp, clear dawn after a December night's snowstorm. This book is about time, and change, and light.

Like any collection of photography, *Seasons* is also about perspective. But not merely the perspective of looking at things from particular angles or elevations. It is about seeing those things—often familiar things—in sometimes fresh and novel ways. To use a Madison Avenue paradox, it's about seeing things again for the first time.

For nearly a decade now, I've photographed the people and places of Williamsburg, working in time with the sun, in concert with the weather, in tune with the light, in harmony with the months. I've neither seen nor shot the same thing twice. Each perspective, every moment, each light, presents something new to my eye, and to the lens, and to the season.

Each Williamsburg scene has a myriad of faces. A whole garden's charm and beauty may be captured in a close-up of a single dew-damp tulip. But its appeal and elegance can be as well, if differently, appreciated in a bird's-eye view that portrays the swaths of its contrasting colors and the unity of its design. The same subject, different perceptions, very different perspectives.

The commonplace zigzag fence that snakes along the boundary of Robertson's Windmill becomes, from the sky, a counterpoint in an aerial composition of before unnoticed grace. Across town, at street level, the blur of a rail fence in the background hurries a costumed woman into an endless instant.

Moving between the details and the panoramas, I look for the interconnectedness of the place. I see the synergy of detail, time, and visual rhythms that make of Williamsburg something more than a collection of buildings.

My ambition is to fix on film the light and the shadow of that something in images suggesting the city's timelessness. That requires, paradoxically, paying attention to my calendar and habitually consulting my clock.

I plan my days by when the dogwoods and redbuds will flower in spring, the redcoats will set up camp in summer, the harvest moons will rise in autumn, and winter cloaks will be donned again on Duke of Gloucester Street.

In hints of yellow among the maples, my eye glimpses the approach of fall, and, in the steam of a carriage-horse's breath, sees its arrival. When holly wreaths begin to garnish Historic Area homes, the day has come once more to think of how to photograph the Grand Illumination fireworks.

By the watch the sun's arc keeps, I can tell just about when the light will be right for the cartouche at the rear of the Governor's Palace. It shows me when to expect to see the first sleepy soldiers stir from the summer tents pitched on Market Square.

The length of summer shadows shows me when the wind will fall and the blossoms will be still on their stalks in the new and ever-changing light of old and immutable Williamsburg.

David M. Doody

The Seasons
in Colonial Virginia

The seasons of the year, with their many variations in climate and appearance of the landscape, have always played a significant, even indispensable, role in people's lives. We moderns perhaps tend to think first of all of the pleasures and delights that each season brings—bursts of spring flowers, lush summer foliage, brilliant autumn colors, the soft whiteness of winter snow. Freed in part by technology from living at the utter mercy of natural forces, we often put out of mind such harsh and forbidding aspects of each season as searing heat, biting cold, drenching rains, or ceaseless drought, although they, too, are an integral part of the cycle of seasons. For peoples who lived at a subsistence level, directly dependent on hunting or agriculture for their very survival, seasons were likely to be appreciated far more for the bounty they provided in good years than for aesthetic qualities. So close was this association in past ages that the very word *season* derives from a Latin term for the act of sowing or planting.

Eighteenth-century Virginians lived closer than we do to the line that divides the darker from the more favorable seasonal manifestations of nature, yet the striking photographs that are the principal feature of this volume provide evidence that our forebears, too, had developed a keen appreciation of the ever-changing beauty of the seasons. The cycle of the seasons continued to shape much in their daily lives, the work that they performed above all, of course, but also their recreation and even their conduct of public affairs, around the differing conditions each season imposed. Virginians lived in a commercial economy capable of providing far more than subsistence alone demanded, yet they grew all their food, apart from a few imported luxuries. Agricultural products, chiefly tobacco and grain, sustained their export economy. Hence they organized much of their routine of work around seasonal cycles of clearing and planting, cultivating, and harvesting.

The first European settlers who came to Virginia in the early seventeenth century found it difficult to cope with the colony's seasonal extremes. What they knew of the newly discovered regions of the world had instilled a fear of genuinely tropical climates, as much as they coveted the products of such regions. The Chesapeake, however, lay in a temperate zone on the same latitude as parts of southern Europe, and they anticipated seasons much like those in England itself. The arrival of the initial group of settlers at

Jamestown in the pleasant spring weather of April and May 1607 seemingly confirmed that expectation. George Percy, one of the leaders of the group, wrote of the "faire meddowes and goodly tall Trees, with such Fresh-waters running through the woods, as I was almost ravished at the first sight thereof." Some days later, he delighted in a walk from Jamestown, observing "all the way as wee went . . . the ground all flowing over with faire flowers of sundry colours and kindes, as though it had been any Garden or Orchard in England."

The truth, however, soon proved different, as the colonists tried to deal with the heat of summer on a low, swampy, insect-infested island. Percy's account now turned to a seemingly endless record of deaths, some from Indian attacks but more from "cruell diseases as Swellings, Fluxes, Burning Fevers" and even more from "meere Famine." Others described similar hardships in the cold winters, especially the ill-fated "Starving Time" of 1609–1610. Although those who survived tended to blame either hostile Indians or their own indolence for their failure, the colonists had also found the summers and winters more extreme than those at home and the largely uncleared land at first inhospitable to traditional European crops and raising domesticated livestock.

The determined colonists hung on, however desperately at first, and then the colony began to grow, thanks to continuing migration from England rather than natural increase. A persistently high death rate among both immigrants and the newborn led Virginians to give a new meaning to the word *season*. It became commonplace to speak of the necessity, if one were to survive, of undergoing "seasoning," whereby new arrivals likely passed through a series of illnesses and, if fortunate, managed to live. They learned, too, by the

manner of constructing and siting their houses, modifying their dress, and adapting their style of life in other respects, to live more comfortably in the greater extremes of a Virginia summer and winter.

The settlers also developed a system of agriculture that borrowed in part from the Indians by growing New World crops, especially corn and tobacco, and by employing Indian methods of farming that made it easier to bring heavily forested lands under cultivation. At the same time, Virginians never abandoned their intention to grow familiar European crops, plant gardens and orchards, and pasture their livestock rather than allowing them to roam freely in the forests. Although the colonists established a way of life based on an agriculture that was shaped by experience to accord more realistically with the climate, land, and seasonal cycles of Virginia, they also attempted to give the countryside a more cultivated and satisfying appearance.

Such a process of accommodation took time, of course, and proceeded unevenly according to specific persons and places. By about the beginning of the eighteenth century, it had reached a point of fruition exemplified in Robert Beverley's *History and Present State of Virginia*, first published in 1705. Beverley was of the first generation of his family to have been born in the colony. While the *History* in some respects unabashedly promoted his native Virginia and glossed over any shortcomings, it captured a state of mind that had developed very widely among Virginians. Recognizing that in its first years the colony had suffered from "the infinite Difficulties and Dangers, that attend a New Settlement," Beverley maintained that "after the advantages of the Climate, and the fruitfulness of the Soil were well known," circumstances had improved.

So far as climate was concerned, Beverley found Virginia to be "in a very happy Situation, between the extreams of Heat and Cold, but inclining rather to the first." He asserted, "I don't know any *English* Plant, Grain or Fruit, that miscarries in *Virginia.*" Conceding that summer did present the "Annoyances and Inconveniences" of "Thunder, Heat, and troublesome Vermin," Beverley blamed those who came from England and insisted on "sweltering about in their thick Cloaths all the Summer" for the bad reputation the season had acquired. He praised the colony in terms he no doubt meant to apply to all the seasons apart from winter:

> I believe it is as healthy a Country, as any under Heaven. . . . Here they enjoy all the benefits of a warm Sun, and by their shady Groves, are protected from its Inconvenience. Here all their Senses are entertain'd with an endless Succession of Native Pleasures. Their Eyes are ravished with the Beauties of naked Nature.

"Winters," he added, "are very short, and don't continue above three or four Months, of which they have seldom thirty days of unpleasant Weather, all the rest being blest with a clear Air, and a bright Sun."

Beverley set a standard of appreciation for the productivity of the land and the moderation and beauties of the seasons in Virginia that natives and visitors alike repeated during the rest of the colonial era. Hugh Jones, who remained in Virginia from 1717 to 1721 as a faculty member at the College of William and Mary, found "the spring and fall are not unlike those seasons in England, only the air is never long foggy, nor very cloudy; but clear." He continued, "The months of December, January, and February are generally much colder, and June, July, and August are much hotter than in England; though sometimes 'tis on a sudden very cool in summer, and pretty warm in winter."

Arriving in Williamsburg in the summer of 1759, Andrew Burnaby likewise praised the moderation of the Virginia seasons:

> The climate is extremely fine, though subject to violent heats in the summer . . . The other seasons, however, make ample amends for this inconvenience: for the autumns and springs are delightful; and the winters are so mild and serene (though there are now and then excessively cold days) as scarcely to require a fire.

Burnaby did note the sudden changes in the weather in all seasons and the frequent and sometimes violent summer thunderstorms. But he found the quantity and variety of trees, fruits, and flowers so great that "one may reasonably assert that no country ever appeared with greater elegance or beauty."

The establishment of Williamsburg as

the new capital of the colony in 1699 coincided with the development among Virginians of a heightened sense that nature in its seasonal guises might be beautiful no less than bountiful, a source of aesthetic enjoyment as much as an unyielding taskmaster through all seasons for those who labored in the soil. Perhaps the carefully drawn plan for the town unconsciously expressed such an assumption in its precise layout of buildings and streets and generous allocation of open green space. As Williamsburg grew, its extensive pleasure gardens greatly enhanced opportunities for at least more affluent residents to enjoy the landscape through the seasons of the year. Town life, too, must have altered and to some extent reduced seasonal influences on work. Those engaged in governance

or in the operation of shops and stores might experience seasonal variations in the amount of work to be done, while craftsmen and artisans might find that some tasks could be better performed in a warmer or colder season. Unlike those in agriculture, such seasonal demands were perhaps more often a matter of convenience than necessity.

The population of Williamsburg remained small throughout the eighteenth century, and it never lost something of the character of a semi-rural community. A significant part of the open spaces remained devoted to kitchen gardens, orchards, and pasturage. Working plantations and farms continued to exist in close proximity to the town. Much of its political and economic activity remained closely tied to the agricultural pursuits of the whole colony and to the rural population it served. Although the passing seasons might in some respects take on a differing aspect in Williamsburg, the capital never became entirely divorced from the seasonal rhythms of eighteenth-century rural life in Virginia.

Winter snow and ice and summer heat and thunderstorms apart, it must have been a combination that made Williamsburg appealing in all the seasons—certainly the photographs in this volume make it seem so. Their contribution is in reality twofold. As photographs taken in the restored Williamsburg of our own day, they record the many ways in which the townsite, its buildings, and the costumed interpreters of Colonial Williamsburg enhance our understanding of life in the colonial era. They also make it possible to draw from them a narrative that calls attention more explicitly to the impact of the seasons on those who lived in eighteenth-century Williamsburg and the manner in which the passage of the seasons shaped many aspects of their lives, whether at work or play.

Springtime in Williamsburg

Springtime is by all odds the favorite season of the year for those who live in Williamsburg today or come to visit, an observation that no doubt applies equally to eighteenth-century residents and travelers. One of the town's best-known colonial visitors, Benjamin Franklin, who came in 1756 to receive the first honorary degree awarded by the College of William and Mary, found Virginia "a pleasant Country, now in full Spring."

Most observers of a Williamsburg spring were less restrained in their enthusiasm than Ben Franklin. The 1774 *Virginia Almanack* extravagantly proclaimed: "At this Season Lady Flora clothes our Grandam Earth with a new Livery, diapered with various Flowers, and checkered with most delightful Objects. . . . Now Shepherds pipe merrily for the Departure of Winter; the Nightengales sing the Sun asleep, and a wild, but charming Chorus, is echoed from every Bough." Nor were the printers of the *Almanack* alone in assigning first place to "Lady Flora" as the harbinger of spring. Then and now, a variety of bulbs and flowers, such as the tulips in full bloom in the Blue Bell garden *(overleaf)*, are one of the loveliest features of Williamsburg's numerous pleasure gardens at the beginning of spring.

Others found a greater beauty in flowering or leafing trees, such as the beeches that frame a gate in the extensive formal gardens at the Governor's Palace *(right)*. St. George Tucker, lawyer and friend of Jefferson, developed one of Williamsburg's most notable post-Revolutionary gardens at his home on Nicholson Street near Palace green. While he liked flowers, Tucker left much of their care to his wife, Lelia, whom he once termed the "Matron of the Green," concentrating attention instead on his beloved trees, especially the fruit orchard. In an enthusiastic comment, Tucker listed seven varieties of fruit trees whose blossoms had all appeared within a single week one spring. Williamsburg's most famous gardener, John Custis, observed that "fine flowers . . . like all delightful things, are very short lived; now fine trees are not only very entertaining but permanent; so I think are to bee prefered."

With the return of spring, farmers and planters hastened to prepare and plant their fields. Josiah Quincy, a young New England lawyer who disdained much of what he found on a trip through Virginia in the spring of 1773, made an exception for the "excellent farms and charming large cleared tracts well-fenced and tilled that are all around me." Spring also stepped up the pace of work for Williamsburg shopkeepers and merchants and those who performed the ordinary labor of the town.

As might be expected of the buildings and grounds that symbolized the authority of the British Crown in the royal colony of Virginia, the gardens of the Governor's Palace were the most elaborate in the capital—and surely one of the best places to savor the full glory of a Williamsburg spring. Governor Alexander Spotswood was primarily responsible for their layout, although work was already under way when he arrived in 1710 and continued after he withdrew from the project following a quarrel with the members of the General Assembly over mounting costs.

(Above) One of the most popular features of the garden for modern visitors is the maze, which is constructed of American holly and modeled on one at Hampton Court Palace outside London. It is seen here from atop the mount, a frequent accompaniment to mazes in English gardens. The mount is an excellent spot from which to see into the maze and across the garden in early spring before the trees are in full leaf.

(Right) White tulips in bloom are a spring feature of the Palace Garden as they are of many in Williamsburg.

(Left) An aerial view of the Palace from the front clearly shows the formal gardens in the forecourt and behind the Ballroom on the rear of the main building. Other areas were devoted to more informal pleasure gardens, a bowling green, and kitchen and fruit gardens.

(Right) Bruton Parish Church served Williamsburg and part of the surrounding area as a parish of the established Church of England. Easter and Whitsunday, or Pentecost, two major holy days of the Anglican calendar, occur in the spring.

(Above) The General Court, the highest court of the colony for both civil and criminal cases, and the General Assembly, the legislature, met in the Capitol. It was likely to be especially busy in the spring. One of the two annual sessions of the General Court occurred in April, drawing large numbers of people to Williamsburg for "Publick Times."

(Left) This view of the home of George Wythe, Thomas Jefferson's law teacher and a signer of the Declaration of Independence, gives an overview of the extensive grounds of a larger Williamsburg residence that included gardens, orchard, pasture, and numerous outbuildings. Spring brought a round of planting and gardening, care of animals and fowl, and related work to households like Wythe's, reminding visitors today of the semirural character of the town.

Spring might step up the pace of work in Williamsburg, but the season could just as well invite the master or a journeyman at the Golden Ball, the shop of James Craig, jeweler and silversmith, to pause and contemplate the beauty of a fine spring day *(above)* or a young boy of the town to drag a stick along a fence for pure pleasure *(right)*.

(Below) Prentis and Company, one of Williamsburg's leading general stores, is busy with the arrival of customers, the delivery of goods by wagon, and a "peep show" to attract passersby.

Close-ups feature three spring flowers: a yellow tulip *(left)*, an iris *(below)*, and a sweet William *(bottom center)*.

(Left) The variety of flowers in the Blue Bell and other Williamsburg gardens seems almost infinite. A recent list of annuals, perennials, biennials, and bulbs planted in the gardens numbers about two hundred varieties, almost all native to the New World or introduced before 1780.

17

Williamsburg's considerable animal population played a part, too, in the round of spring activities. *(Above and left)* Red and Clay, two Milking Devon oxen, are being worked in a field behind the Benjamin Waller House. Devon cattle, now rare, are a versatile breed that produce milk for dairy products and beef for food and have great strength as draft animals. *(Right)* Corn, wheat, and tobacco crops were vital to the economy of eighteenth-century Virginia and were cultivated near the town. In this scene, a wheat crop is already well advanced in one field, while the oxen are being employed to prepare another for planting.

Gamboling lambs and newly sheared
sheep are a certain sign of spring. The
sheep are English Leicesters that have, in
the best eighteenth-century manner, been
hand sheared.

(Above) The extensive working area behind the George Wythe House includes a sizable area for raising fowl. The rear of the main house can be seen beyond the Fattening Coop. A part of the Fowl House is visible on the right.

(Above and left) Dung fowl at the Wythe House.

(Left) An American Cream mare with her foal graze against the backdrop of a dogwood tree in full spring bloom. *(Below)* Blown pale yellow lily-flowered tulips in the Governor's Palace garden.

Brick was a favored material for Benjamin
Powell, a successful Williamsburg contractor
who built a brick home for himself and his family
in town *(above)*. Powell also repaired the Public
Gaol, the Capitol, and the Palace and built the
Public Hospital and the tower and steeple at
Bruton Parish Church *(left)*. After a spring rain,
puddles linger on the ground behind the Isham
Goddin Shop *(right)*.

Gardens in eighteenth-century Williamsburg tended to be trimmed and fenced, despite a trend toward more natural looks in English gardens of the period. *(Right)* The backyard of Hartwell Perry's ordinary. Perry operated an ordinary, as taverns were sometimes called, from the mid-1780s until he died about 1800.

Late spring can occasionally bring snow, which covers tulips blooming on the grounds of the Governor's Palace. The colony's House of Burgesses criticized Governor Alexander Spotswood for "lavishing away" funds on the garden's canal *(above)*, which the burgesses called a "fish pond."

Summertime in Williamsburg

Summer was a difficult, unhealthy season in Tidewater Virginia. Even though observers sought to put the best possible face on it, they had to admit that "violent heats" and "frequent and violent gusts, with thunder and lightning," occurred with regularity. In a conversation with Philip Fithian, tutor to the children of Robert Carter of Nomini Hall, Frances Tasker Carter, mistress of the plantation, declared fall to be her favorite season, not so much for its own sake but because it relieved the "Anxiety & Pain" and the "Thunder & Lightning & intense Heat" of summer. Fithian favored summer when "the world around us is beautiful & growing to necessary perfection." After Fithian spent his first July and August at Nomini Hall, filling much of his diary with accounts of the many hot and stormy days and an endless series of illnesses that he and the family suffered, the tutor might well have agreed with Mrs. Carter.

No matter how oppressive summers were, work had to go on during a critical time for the cultivation of corn and tobacco and for harvesting early grain crops. In Williamsburg, the pace of public life slowed, although craftsmen might use the longer hours of daylight to advantage. More pleasant days occurred often enough for people to enjoy the summer pleasures often mentioned in diaries and letters—among them "fish-feasts," boat trips, expeditions to pick berries, horse races, and, above all, walking in the gardens, including those at the Governor's Palace *(overleaf)*. Summer afforded, too, the best opportunity to enjoy the bounty of gardens and orchards *(left)*.

(Above) On this summer day, the keeper of the Public Gaol gives his son a lesson in the art of whittling. Perhaps the Court of Oyer and Terminer, which heard major criminal cases, had concluded its regular June session, leaving the keeper with no prisoners in his charge and time to relax.

(Below) A view of the front grounds of the Benjamin Waller House, home of a prominent Williamsburg attorney who was George Wythe's law teacher, highlights the lush summer greenery of the town. *(Right)* The variety of Williamsburg fences rivals that of the gardens they enclose. In this case, the haze and humidity that envelops them also captures perfectly a typical Williamsburg summer day. *(Below right)* China asters in summer bloom along a fence at the Grissell Hay Lodging House.

Workmen are readying the ornate carriage for a summer outing by the royal governor *(above top)*, while a youth rolls his hoop, enjoying a timeless form of play *(above)*. The two-wheeled riding chair traversing a country road would have been an equally common sight on the streets of the capital *(right)*. Thanks to archaeology and a surviving sketch, the Benjamin Waller House garden is one of the best documented as well as most beautiful in Williamsburg *(overleaf)*.

The residents of Williamsburg seldom encountered soldiers in their town apart from local militia musters that more often were social occasions rather than serious military exercises. Scenes of a summer encampment by a British military reenactment are a reminder that the onset of the American Revolution altered their lives. In the summer of 1781, British forces under Lord Cornwallis occupied Williamsburg without resistance. Earlier in the year, a smaller force entered Williamsburg briefly, exchanging fire with a volunteer company of students from the college. *(Overleaf)* The "redcoats" firing their weapons recall that little-known incident. The town was also a scene of American military activity, most notably on the eve of the Battle of Yorktown in late summer 1781, but also earlier when Patriot volunteers who formed a nucleus of the first Virginia regiments began to assemble at Williamsburg late in the summer of 1775.

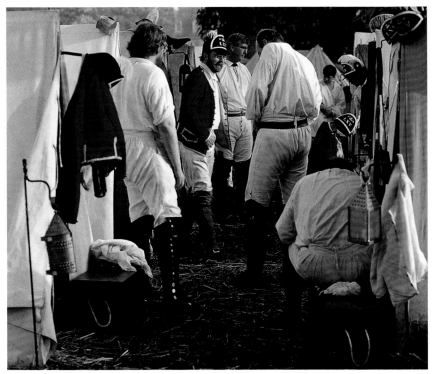

Brickmaking provides an excellent example of
Williamsburg artisans at work in the summer.
A few brick structures were standing on the site
of Williamsburg prior to the establishment of the
new capital in 1699. As the town grew, the
demand for bricks increased greatly. These
scenes depict artisans at work at the Carpenter's
and Brickmaker's Yard at the corner of
Nicholson and Botetourt Streets. In the
eighteenth century, bricks were often made at or
near actual building sites.

The steps in
brickmaking include
treading the clay
mixture *(far left)*,
firing the kiln *(left)*,
and stacking the
bricks *(below)*.

Nowhere was summer more demanding than in the cultivation of tobacco and grains on Virginia plantations. Tobacco in particular required close attention. All but the smallest farms depended to a large extent on slaves, male and female, for hard work in the fields. Workers shouldering their hoes or other hand tools and walking to or from the fields were a typical sight. There was work to be done, usually by older women, in the slave quarter as well. Larger plantations likely had a few skilled slave artisans working at crafts such as carpentry, shoemaking, or blacksmithing.

Autumn in Williamsburg

Although autumn, like spring, was generally accounted one of the finer seasons of the year, colonists almost seemed to take it for granted, seldom celebrating the startling beauty of fall colors as we do today. Some, like Frances Tasker Carter, liked autumn simply because it brought an end to summer miseries. Robert Carter, her husband, explained that he, too, preferred fall since "he supposed that in these Months the Air is more uniform and settled than in any other so long time in the year"—a view that seems more practical than aesthetic.

Scenes of the Peyton Randolph House, home of the longtime attorney general of the colony, Speaker of the House of Burgesses, and president of the first Continental Congress *(overleaf)*, a carriage and colorful trees on Palace green *(upper left)*, the James Geddy Foundry *(lower left)*, and a row of houses and shops near the Capitol on Duke of Gloucester Street *(right)* capture another aspect of the season—the feeling of serenity that an autumn in Williamsburg often conveys.

Autumn in the eighteenth-century capital was just as likely to bustle with activities as many of the following photographs suggest. Those who came for Publick Times thronged the area around the Capitol. Their presence made fall a busy time for merchants and craftsmen, while in the countryside,

planters faced the demanding task of readying their tobacco for market. Regardless of good weather or bad, colonists could not have postponed these activities. Despite occasional storms, the generally temperate and even qualities of the autumn weather made the work easier and more inviting. Robert Carter's attitude may be typical of the favorable, yet restrained, manner in which many Virginians responded to fall.

Colorful autumn leaves have begun to fall, and there is a hint of briskness in the
air in these scenes of a carriage turning the corner at the Prentis House *(above left)*,
men conversing over a fence at the Anderson Blacksmith Shop *(below, far left)*,
customers entering the Margaret Hunter Millinery Shop *(left)*, and a carter
unloading new merchandise at the Prentis Store *(above)*.

The Capitol of the colony was likely to be especially busy in the autumn. By late in the season in a typical year, planters had largely finished curing their tobacco and found fall a convenient time to come to Williamsburg on personal or public business. The General Court held one of its two annual sessions in October. The General Assembly, which was convened at the pleasure of the governor, frequently met in the fall too. Sessions might last from only a few days to several weeks, although autumn sessions were sometimes lengthy, extending through November and almost to Christmas. The scenes in the Hall of the House of Burgesses, the lower, elected branch of the Assembly, depict members engaged in vigorous debate in session and relaxing during a recess.

(Left) The cupola of the Capitol displays two impressive symbols of the authority of Great Britain in Virginia—the British Union Jack flying above and the royal coat of arms at the base. *(Above)* The heated gathering on the steps of a nearby tavern re-creates one of the first hostile acts against that authority in the controversy that led to revolution and independence. On November 1, 1765, the hated Stamp Act against which Virginia and other colonies had been protesting for several months was scheduled to go into effect. George Mercer, the Virginian appointed to oversee the sale of the stamps in the colony, arrived from England on October 29 and the next day made his way to Williamsburg, which was crowded with people in town for the session of the General Court. Met by an angry gathering that included many "Gentlemen of Property," Mercer sought out the royal governor, Francis Fauquier, who conducted him to safety. Fearing further violence, Mercer resigned the next day, his reputation in Virginia permanently destroyed. The General Court and the county courts as well ceased sitting on civil cases rather than use the required stamps on legal documents. Virginians had evaded British laws in the past; for the first time, they openly defied one.

(Above) The shoemaker has replenished the woodpile at his shop in preparation for the colder weather ahead. (Right) On a bright autumn day a man casts a long shadow against a fence at the Roscow Cole House.

(Above) The Benjamin Powell House was constructed in the 1760s by the successful building contractor responsible for such structures as the tower of Bruton Parish Church and the Public Hospital. In autumn its ornamental garden fronting Waller Street features brilliant red foliage of dogwood and crape myrtle. The area to the rear of the house and garden contains numerous outbuildings and a work yard, kitchen garden, and pasture. *(Overleaf)* A view across the kitchen garden looking toward the rear of the Benjamin Powell House provides another perspective on its sizable complex of utilitarian buildings and work spaces that characterized larger town properties like Mr. Powell's.

(Left) Williamsburg gunsmiths found autumn a more comfortable season in which to work at a forge. *(Above)* A modern gunsmith at Colonial Williamsburg crafted this rifle in the English fowler style. Such weapons were important to eighteenth-century Virginians for hunting and for service in the militia, which was required of most able-bodied men.

Tobacco has been aptly described as a crop that required attention and work in every month of the year. Some of the most critical phases of that work had to be accomplished in autumn. Tobacco generally ripened in late August or in September. Growers cut the plants *(far left)*, cured the leaves in special barns, stemmed them, and prized the leaves firmly into hogsheads for shipment to England and Scotland *(left)*. Each part of the process required careful judgment and expert knowledge *(below)* as the work went on throughout the autumn. It had to be completed if possible before the weather turned cold and damaged this vital cash crop.

Except for free time on Sundays
and rare holidays, slaves worked
hard through all the seasons. The
late autumn may have afforded
some relief from the most
demanding forms of field labor,
however. *(Left)* On a fall night in
a slave quarter, a slave carpenter
teaches his son the trade, a skill
that might get the young man out
of the field and provide a better
life. *(Above)* With the permission
of a master—or sometimes without
it—slaves found occasions for
music, dancing, and their own
social life in the quarter.

Wintertime in Williamsburg

Although no one likely thought winter the best of seasons, colonists and travelers alike consistently emphasized its mildness. They conceded its unpredictability, with alternating periods of bitter cold and warm, sunny days with brilliant skies. The fair weather, mild or frigid, was interspersed, too, with rain, ice, and snow, although snows usually melted quickly. Thomas Jefferson kept a record of temperatures in Williamsburg for the five years 1772–1777. The average low temperature for the winter months never dropped below freezing, standing at 38.5 degrees in the coldest month of January. He noted that periods of extraordinary cold did occur, including a 6 degree reading at Williamsburg in January 1780, when people walked across the ice on the York River.

In January 1774, Philip Fithian, tutor to the children of Robert Carter of Nomini Hall, listed no fewer than six major changes in the weather, half involving snow, ice, or intense cold. Although none of the family attended church on two of the most disagreeable Sundays, weather did not deter them from a busy round of balls and dinners. Fithian and one of the Carter sons rode horseback for exercise and pleasure, once in snow. Some of the family went ice skating on nearby millponds. If a month of reasonably bad weather interfered so little with the life of a rural plantation, citizens of Williamsburg must certainly have kept up their usual activities, only moving more of them indoors. The town was quietest in winter when Williamsburg took on more of the character of a small community and appeared less the capital of Britain's largest and most populous colony.

The Christmas season that looms so large in the present day had a counterpart of sorts in the eighteenth century, yet significant differences existed as well. While colonial Virginians enthusiastically celebrated the season, observance began only on Christmas Day itself and extended through the Twelve Days of Christmas to the Feast of the Epiphany on January 6. Decorations were simpler, mostly unadorned local greens and pungent herbs placed inside the houses and the church. Traditional feasting was customary, but small presents were confined to small gifts from masters and parents to dependent children, apprentices, servants, and slaves. Whatever the differences, then as now, Christmas was a high point of the winter season in Williamsburg.

(Overleaf) The Wythe House and its dependencies are blanketed under an unusually heavy snowfall. *(Above left)* A musician plays a baroque guitar in Chowning's Tavern on a winter night. *(Right)* The Sign of the Rhinoceros displays modern decorations.

(Left) While not strictly Christmas lighting, a cresset being refueled at the Mary Dickinson Store adjoining the James Geddy House casts a bright glow on a winter night. Soft candlelight gleaming from every window adds as much to the holiday spirit in the Historic Area today as do the wreaths and other Christmas greens on every building. Three modest but brightly lit dwellings on Francis Street include The Quarter, a cottage believed to have been at one time a slave residence (above), and the Moody House, owned by a Scottish merchant, and the Ewing House, home of a blacksmith (overleaf).

(Above) William Prentis, one of the town's most prosperous merchants and civic leaders, lived in this substantial house a block away from his store. *(Right)* Even such utilitarian spaces as the kitchen and its surrounding yard at the Roscow Cole House take on a certain beauty in a light snow. The woodpile is a reminder of the great winter demand for firewood in an eighteenth-century household—even one not as grand as Nomini Hall plantation, where Philip Fithian noted that a cart drawn by three pairs of oxen delivered four loads of wood daily to supply twenty-eight fires.

In the wintertime, Williamsburg residents retreated indoors for much of their work and recreation. Shoemaker George Wilson had sufficient business in 1773 so that he advertised for two or three journeymen to assist him at his shop near the Greenhow Store on Duke of Gloucester Street. The shoemakers busily at work by candlelight suggest that Wilson was successful *(above)*. Christmas provided a special occasion for indoor social festivities, here enlivened by a musician playing a now rare but much favored eighteenth-century instrument, the glass harmonica *(right)*.

While winter encouraged more indoor activity, perhaps a cooper did not begrudge the need to perform some work in the cold, since the heat required for shaping staves into a barrel also kept him warm.

The royal governor and his guests would have avoided the wintry Palace gardens, in which the tall yaupon holly topiary looked especially stark, leaving the enjoyment of the prospect to the geese and ducks gathered by an unfrozen section of the garden canal (*overleaf*).

To mark the Christmas
season at the College of
William and Mary today,
students observe the old
English custom of
bringing in a yule log to
burn in the fireplace of the
Great Hall in the historic
Wren Building. In the
earliest years of the
college, the boys of the
Grammar School adopted
another English tradition
by locking themselves in a
room until the president
and masters agreed to
begin the Christmas
holiday early. The mock
confrontation ended with
refreshments all around,
except for one year when
the students caused a
ruckus by firing pistols
loaded with powder but
no shot through the doors.

Colonial Virginians
often celebrated Christmas
by firing guns. Tutor
Fithian noted being
awakened on Christmas
morning in 1773 by "Guns
firing all around the
House." The fireworks
that are a favorite part of
the holiday celebrations in
Williamsburg today
preserve something of the
same festive spirit that our
forefathers so enjoyed
(overleaf).